Beluga Whales

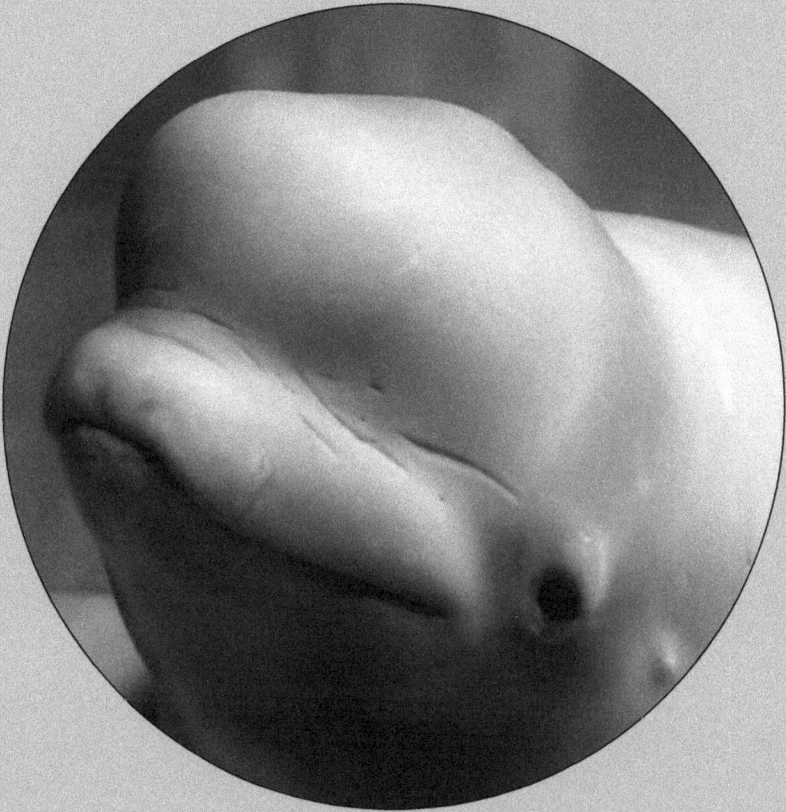

Victoria Blakemore

Copyright info/picture credits

Cover, Luna Vandoorne/AdobeStock; Page 3, Andrea Izzotti/AdobeStock; Page 5, Isalazar/AdobeStock; Page 7, dejavu-designs/AdobeStock; Page 9, mur162/AdobeStock; Pages 10-11, Patrick Poendl/AdobeStock; Page 13, Chee-Onn Leong/AdobeStock; Page 15, dejavudesigns/AdobeStock; Page 17, Cristian Irranca/AdobeStock; Page 19, tpsdave/Pixabay; Page 21, Julie Clopper/AdobeStock; Page 23; Wollwerth Imagery/AdobeStock; Page 25, Christopher Meder/AdobeStock; Page 27, Vladimir Wrangel/AdobeStock; Page 29, Cristian Irranca/AdobeStock; Page 31, chbaum/AdobeStock; Page 33, Wollwerth Imagery/AdobeStock; Page 35, Luna Vandoorne/AdobeStock

Table of Contents

What Are Beluga Whales?

Beluga whales are large marine mammals. They are a kind of toothed whale. Beluga whales are in the same family as narwhals.

Beluga whales are sometimes called "white whales" because of their color.

Size

Beluga whales are smaller in length than many other whales. They can grow to be about fifteen feet long.

Most adult beluga whales weigh between 2,500 and 3,500 pounds. Males are larger than females.

Beluga whales have a lot

more **blubber**, or fat, than

other whales.

Physical Characteristics

Beluga whales have a very

streamlined shape. They do

not have a **dorsal fin** like

some other whales.

Belugas have two **pectoral**

fins. They help the beluga

whale to steer. Their tail fin

helps to **propel** them through

the water.

6

Belugas have a round head. The round part in the front is called the melon. A beluga's melon is soft and can change shape.

Habitat

Beluga whales are usually found in the cold waters of the Arctic ocean and the seas around it.

Some belugas **migrate** south when it gets colder. Others stay in one area all year.

Range

Beluga whales are only found in the Arctic Circle. The Arctic Circle is the area of icy water and land around the North Pole.

10

Beluga whales are found around Canada, Greenland, northern Europe, and Asia.

II

Diet

Like other toothed whales,

belugas are **carnivores**. They

eat only meat.

Their diet is made up of fish,

shrimp, crabs, squid, octopus,

and snails. Most of the time,

they will eat whatever they

can find.

Beluga whales do most of their

hunting for food on the ocean

floor.

Beluga whales have a special way of finding food on the ocean floor. They blow water into the sand to find prey that is hiding.

Belugas also hunt schools of fish. They work as a team to herd the fish into one area before catching them.

Beluga whales do not chew

their food. They swallow it

whole.

Communication

Beluga whales use sound to communicate. They have been known to chirp, squeal, whistle, and cluck.

Beluga whales are often called the "canaries of the sea." This is because they make many different chirping sounds.

Beluga whales can be loud.

They can often be heard

above the water.

Echolocation

Beluga whales use something called echolocation to find their way and look for food.

Echolocation is when an animal makes a clicking sound and listens for it to bounce off of objects. Beluga whales use that echo to know where things are.

Echolocation helps beluga

whales to find holes in the ice.

Movement

Beluga whales swim more

slowly than many other whales.

They usually swim about five

miles per hour.

Belugas do not usually dive

very deep. They aren't seen

deeper than about sixty feet

below the ocean's surface

very often.

Beluga whales are one of the

few kinds of whales that can

swim backwards.

Pod Life

Beluga whales are very social animals. They live in groups that are called pods.

Pods are made up of between two and twenty-five whales. Most pods have about ten whales.

Pods hunt, travel, and play

together.

Beluga Whale Calves

Beluga whales have one baby. Baby beluga whales are called calves. They are born gray in color.

Calves stay with their mothers for at least the first two years of their lives.

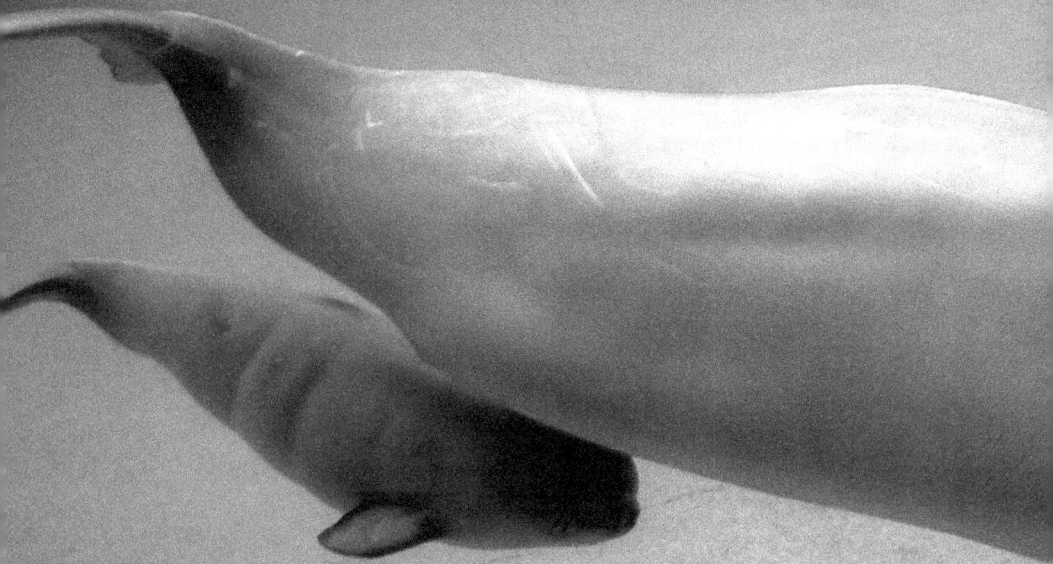

Mothers and calves often

form their own pod until the

calves are older.

Theme Parks

Beluga whales are kept at some aquariums and theme parks. They are very intelligent and can be trained to do tricks.

Some people believe that beluga whales should not be kept in theme parks.

Beluga whales in theme parks

are often given things to play

with.

Life Span

In the wild, beluga whales are believed to live between thirty and fifty years. It can be hard for researchers to tell for sure.

In **captivity**, beluga whales usually live less than thirty years.

Beluga whales that live in captivity may not live as long as they would have in the wild.

Population

Beluga whales are listed as near threatened. They are not **endangered**, but their populations have been **declining**.

There are believed to be more than 150,000 beluga whales left in the wild.

Pollution, rising temperatures, and hunting are threats that beluga whales are facing.

Helping Beluga Whales

Pollution is a problem for belugas in some places. People are trying to get companies to stop polluting the water with chemicals.

Beluga whales have been hunted for many years. There are laws to protect belugas from being hunted.

Temperatures in the Arctic have been getting warmer. This is not good for beluga whales.

There are groups that are trying to help belugas. They want to try to stop the change in temperature so that habitats are not destroyed.

Glossary

Blubber: fat that keeps animals warm

Captivity: animals that are kept by humans, not in the wild

Carnivore: an animal that eats meat

Declining: getting smaller

Dorsal fin: the large fin on top of many whales

Endangered: at risk of becoming

extinct

Migrate: travel from one place to

another

Pectoral fins: fins that are on the

side of a whale's body

Propel: push forward

Streamlined: smooth surface,

allows for fast movement

through water

About the Author

Victoria Blakemore is a first grade

teacher in Southwest Florida with a

passion for reading.

You can visit her at

www.elementaryexplorers.com

Also in This Series

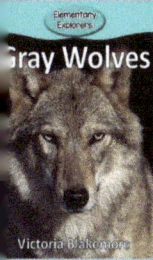

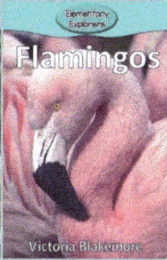

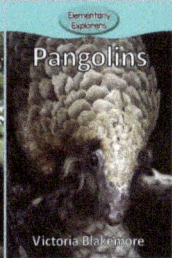

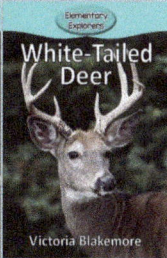

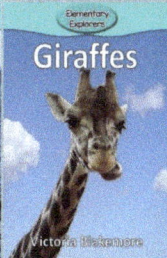

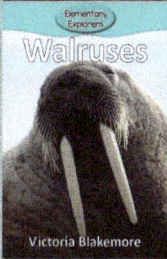

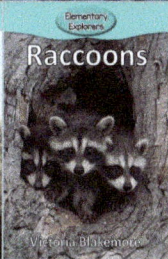

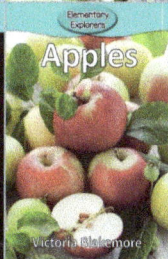

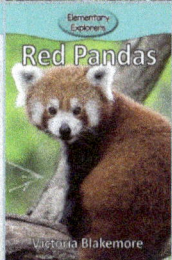

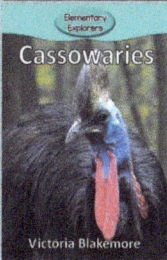

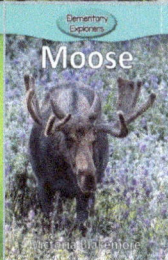

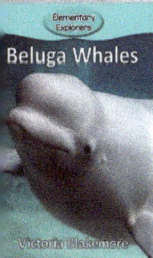

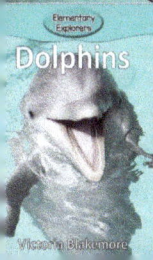

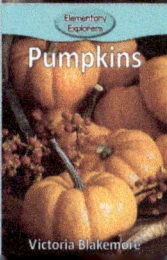

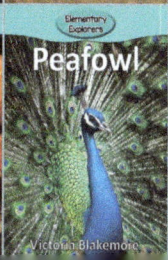

Gray Wolves	Sloths	Flamingos	Camels	Koalas	Honey Bees
Pandas	Pangolins	White-Tailed Deer	Orcas	Giraffes	Corn
Meerkats	Echidnas	Walruses	Raccoons	Bald Eagles	Apples
Arctic Foxes	Red Pandas	Cassowaries	Tigers	Ladybugs	Moose
Beluga Whales	Leopards	Elephants	Jellyfish	Binturongs	Lions
Dolphins	Reindeer	Hammerhead Sharks	Hippos	Pumpkins	Peafowl

Also in This Series

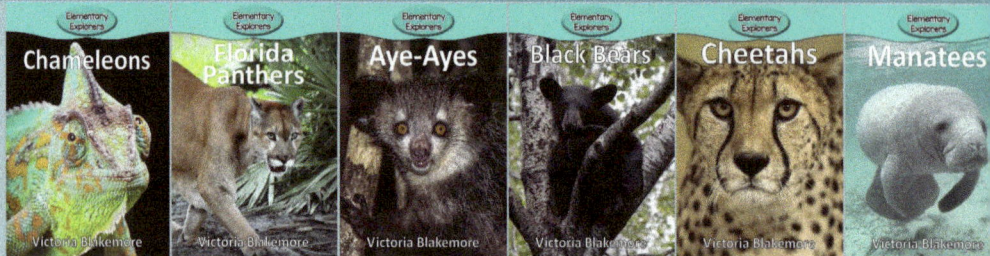

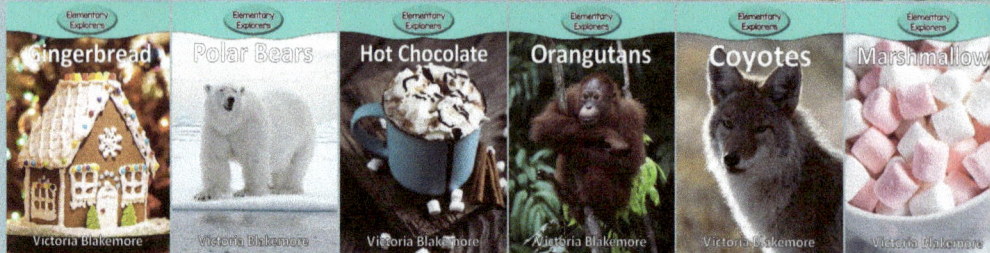

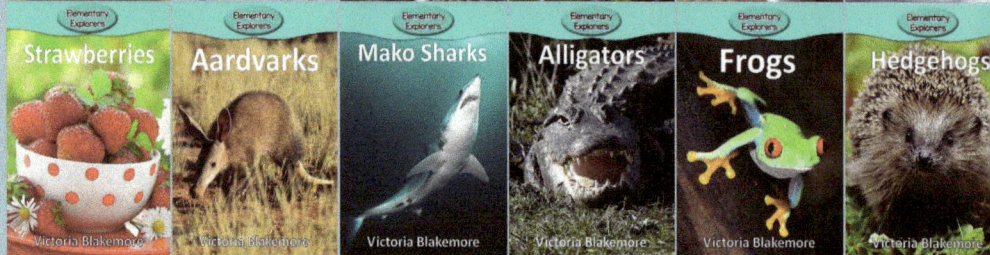

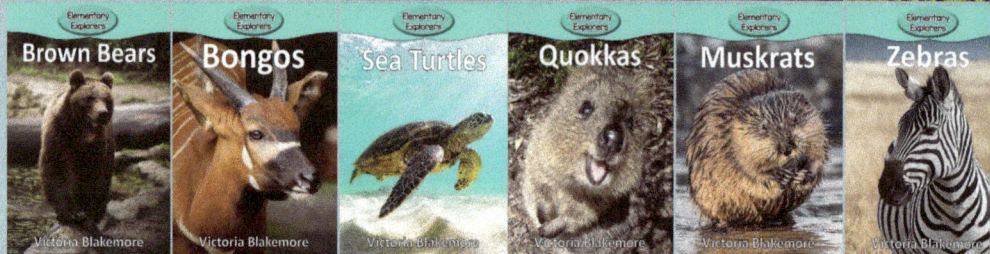

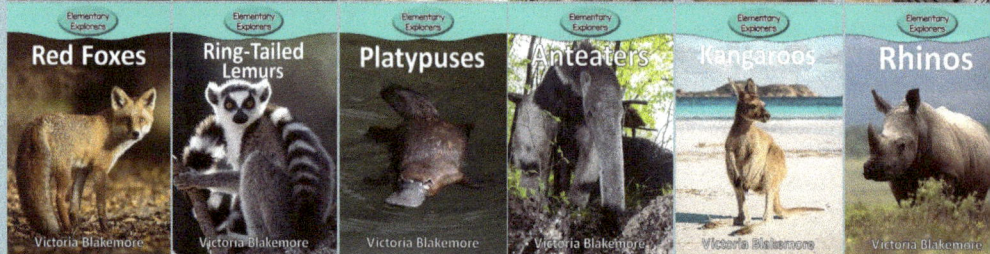

Chameleons	Florida Panthers	Aye-Ayes	Black Bears	Cheetahs	Manatees
Gingerbread	Polar Bears	Hot Chocolate	Orangutans	Coyotes	Marshmallow
Strawberries	Aardvarks	Mako Sharks	Alligators	Frogs	Hedgehogs
Brown Bears	Bongos	Sea Turtles	Quokkas	Muskrats	Zebras
Red Foxes	Ring-Tailed Lemurs	Platypuses	Anteaters	Kangaroos	Rhinos
Jaguars	Wombats				

Elementary Explorers

Victoria Blakemore

www.ingramcontent.com/pod-product-compliance
Lightning Source LLC
Chambersburg PA
CBHW051249020426
42333CB00025B/3136